The Abraham Lincoln Presidential Library and Museum
was created to reach visitors with the story of Abraham Lincoln
and his times. More than fifteen years in the making, it uses
modern technology, imagination, and historical scholarship and
artifacts to present the life of America's greatest president during the
greatest challenge the United States ever faced: the Civil War.

Despite his global legacy, Abraham Lincoln came from humble
beginnings. When asked to provide an autobiographical sketch in
1859, he wrote apologetically: "There is not much of it for the reason,
I suppose, that there is not much of me." The plainspoken Illinois
lawyer could not have imagined that his greatest legacies—preserving
the Union and eliminating slavery—were yet to be realized.

We hope that by learning about Abraham Lincoln's life and
world, you will better understand the freedoms that he helped to
protect—as well as your own role in shaping history.

—The Abraham Lincoln Presidential Library and Museum

Lincoln's Stovepipe Hat: This emblem of the sixteenth
president was purchased from a store on the old square in Springfield,
Illinois, in the 1850s. Made of beaver fur, its brim has marks from
Lincoln's fingers where he continually doffed it to passersby.

Portrait by a Friend: When Reverend Lewis Peter Clover painted Lincoln in Springfield in July 1860, he had known the future president for three years.

ABRAHAM LINCOLN
Presidential Library and Museum

OFFICIAL COMMEMORATIVE GUIDE

BECKON BOOKS

Meet the Lincolns

In the entryway to the Abraham Lincoln Presidential Museum is a life-size replica of the Lincoln family, wearing traveling clothes that evoke the family's trip from Springfield to Washington. The Lincolns' other son, Eddy, died in 1850 at age three. Behind the family on the far back wall is a large mural portrait, *Lincoln in 1860*, by Gregory Manchess. The portrait, seen at right, highlights Lincoln on the eve of his presidential election. Manchess, Danilo Montejo, and Keith Rocco painted eight original murals for the Museum that depict key times in Lincoln's life.

A. Lincoln

❊ An Experience Museum ❊

❊ ❊ ❊

The Abraham Lincoln Presidential Library and Museum educates visitors on the life of America's sixteenth president by using both traditional artifacts and modern technology. The museum is divided into two journeys: Lincoln's pre-presidential years, and his life in the White House. Many of these exhibits re-create scenes from Lincoln's life, such as his Indiana boyhood cabin, which imagines his excitement in learning how to read, and the White House office, where Lincoln and his cabinet members discuss the Emancipation Proclamation. Some of these scenes, including Lincoln's boyhood cabin, are built to their original scale. Original scores by composer David Kneupper, based on Lincoln-era music, are piped in throughout the exhibits.

The museum contains two effects theaters: the Union Theater, where an eighteen-minute movie, *Lincoln's Eyes*, gives an overview of the president's life; and the *Ghosts of the Library* multimedia show, in which a "ghost" explains why libraries and museums collect original materials. A large room for temporary exhibits, the Illinois Gallery, highlights specific topics on Lincoln and his times.

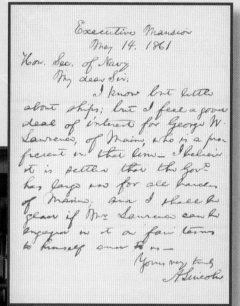

LETTERS AND LIVES
Above: The Abraham Lincoln Presidential Library and Museum owns nearly 1,600 documents in Lincoln's hand, and some are always on display. In this letter, Lincoln recommends George Lawrence of Maine for a naval position.

GHOSTLY VIEWS
Left: The *Ghosts of the Library* show is one of only three in the world to use Holavision™ technology.

SWISS MUSIC BOX
Above: Mary Lincoln's music box is mentioned in *Ghosts of the Library*, and it is also rotated on and off display in the Treasures Gallery.

❊ Did You Know? ❊

The music playing in the plaza—an original score recorded by a symphony orchestra and chorus—is based upon period music that Lincoln liked. In addition, each gallery has its own original audio track. Most are inspired by the quadrille, a favorite dance of the time.

"FELLOW-CITIZENS, *WE* CANNOT ESCAPE HISTORY."

— *Abraham Lincoln, Second Annual Message to Congress, December 1, 1862*

✧ Beginnings ✧

✧ ✧ ✧

Abraham Lincoln was born on February 12, 1809, near Hodgenville, Kentucky. In 1816, his father, Thomas Lincoln, moved the family to Indiana. Lincoln developed a love of books and learning in Indiana. He also learned how to wield an ax, plow fields, and ply the carpenter's trade. Shortly after the family's move, Lincoln's mother, Nancy Hanks Lincoln, died from milk sickness. His father remarried a widow, Sarah Bush Johnston, and the blended family of eight all resided in a one-room cabin that Lincoln had helped his father to build.

Farmers like Thomas Lincoln accounted for 97 percent of the American workforce in the early to mid-1800s. Abraham Lincoln's interests, however, ran in a different direction: toward the emerging professions that served the new market economy, which was driven by commerce and trade. Intrigued by what opportunity lurked beyond frontier life, he took a flatboat to New Orleans in 1828.

Abraham Lincoln was introduced to the French Creole culture in New Orleans—as well as to the sale of slaves that occurred at the city's auction houses each day. He found slavery to be both physically and emotionally inhumane. Unfortunately, slavery was widespread. From 1820 to 1860, one slave was sold on average every 3.6 minutes in America. By the time of his presidential election in 1860, the total slave population was about four million.

THE READER
Above: As a boy in Indiana, Lincoln taught himself to read. *Aesop's Fables* was among the books he borrowed and loved.

SUM BOOK
Right: The oldest piece of writing in Lincoln's hand is this page of long division and homemade rhyming—the first page from his sum book, written when he was about fifteen.

AN HONEST RAILSPLITTER
Above: Lincoln challenged himself with physical as well as mental labor during his Kentucky, Indiana, and early Illinois days, as shown in this 1908 print by J. L. G. Ferris.

"I WAS BORN AND HAVE EVER REMAINED
IN THE MOST HUMBLE WALKS OF LIFE."

— *Abraham Lincoln, in a speech for his first run for the
Illinois House of Representatives, March 9, 1832*

Early Education

Abraham Lincoln's parents were barely literate. He and his sister received about one year of formal education. "When I came of age I did not know much," he recalled. "Somehow, I could read, write, and cipher to the rule of three; but that was all." For Lincoln, books provided a source of information as well as escapism from the rude surroundings of the Indiana frontier. His favorites—most likely borrowed from neighbors—included Aesop's *Fables*, John Bunyan's *The Pilgrim's Progress*, Daniel Defoe's *Robinson Crusoe*, and Parson Weems's *Life and Memorable Actions of George Washington*.

Family Photos

No photograph exists of Abraham and Mary together—or of the whole family. In reality, there are two posed photographs of Abraham and Tad, and one of Mary standing with Willie and Tad. Several engravings were made during and after the presidency that merge separate images into a family scene. Some of these, such as the engraving at right, depict Abraham and Mary, and some include one or more of the children. Robert, the eldest, who attended Harvard College during most of the war, appears least often in these.

⊹ Early Family Life ⊹

Abraham Lincoln moved to New Salem, Illinois, in 1831. He held a variety of jobs there, including storekeeper, militia captain in the Black Hawk War, and postmaster. In 1836, the courts allowed him to practice law. The following year, he moved to Springfield, Illinois, the state's new capital.

Lincoln lived in Springfield for five years before succumbing to the intelligence, wit, and grace of Mary Todd, whom he married in 1842. Raised in Lexington, Kentucky, by wealthy merchant and civic leader Robert Smith Todd, Mary had every advantage that Lincoln lacked—an excellent education, a comfortable life, and training in social etiquette. But they shared a mutual admiration of Henry Clay, a Whig politician and good friend of Mary's father.

Lincoln was able to carve out a comfortable middle-class life for Mary and their four sons with his legal career. The job required him to travel to the other counties in the Eighth Judicial Circuit, taking him from home for months at a time, but Lincoln loved practicing law. To him, the law was a necessary component of a republican government, a way to help people resolve their disputes in a peaceful and reasoned manner. Lincoln argued cases both for and against slave owners, for and against railroads, for and against farmers. He believed that everyone deserved to be represented in the best manner possible.

POSTMASTER LINCOLN
Above left: Thanks to his job as a postmaster, Lincoln knew everyone around New Salem, Illinois. This painting of Lincoln was done by Fletcher C. Ransom in 1942.

SERVING BOWL
Above: A small bowl of Meissen china used by the Lincoln family in Springfield illustrates Mary Lincoln's taste in decorating. The inside ring of green leaves and violets reflects her favorite color: purple.

⊹ Did You Know? ⊹

On April 15, 1837, Lincoln left New Salem and relocated to Springfield, Illinois. He was twenty-eight years old. On this exact date twenty-eight years later, Lincoln would die at age fifty-six. His move to Springfield marked the literal midpoint of his life. This 1846 photograph was the first he sat for.

MAHOGANY VANITY
Right: Mary gave this mahogany bureau-top vanity to her sister Ann. Three of Mary's sisters lived in Springfield.

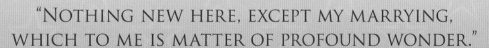

> "NOTHING NEW HERE, EXCEPT MY MARRYING,
> WHICH TO ME IS MATTER OF PROFOUND WONDER."
>
> — *Abraham Lincoln, Letter to Samuel D. Marshall, November 11, 1842*

THE LINCOLN HOME
Above: Abraham, Willie, and Tad (peeking from behind the post) stand in front of the family home in this photo taken in the summer of 1860. At the curb are two neighbors.

THE LAW OFFICE
Right: An engraving of Lincoln and his law partner, William H. Herndon, depicts the two lawyers and a clerk hard at work in the Lincoln–Herndon Law Offices.

NAME PLATE
Right: Before houses were numbered, residents posted their name on a large label next to their front door for the benefit of callers. This one came from the Lincolns' home in Springfield.

"DISCOURAGE LITIGATION. PERSUADE YOUR NEIGHBORS TO COMPROMISE WHENEVER YOU CAN. POINT OUT TO THEM HOW THE NOMINAL WINNER IS OFTEN A REAL LOSER—IN FEES, EXPENSES, AND WASTE OF TIME. AS A PEACEMAKER THE LAWYER HAS A SUPERIOR OPPORTUNITY OF BEING A GOOD MAN. THERE WILL STILL BE BUSINESS ENOUGH."

— *Abraham Lincoln, Notes for a Law Lecture, July 1, 1850*

WILLIE LINCOLN (1850–1862)
Below: Said to take after his father more than the other boys, Willie was well-spoken and kept a watchful eye on his rowdy younger brother, Tad.

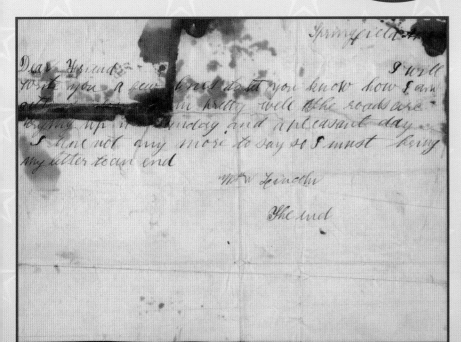

ROBERT LINCOLN (1843–1926)
Above: The oldest Lincoln son, Robert, had a distinguished career in law, politics, diplomacy, and industry. His brother Eddy, the second of the four boys, died in 1850 at age three.

THOMAS "TAD" LINCOLN (1853–1871)
Above: Tad brought life to the White House and became his mother's companion after Abraham's death in 1865. A cleft palate made his speech difficult to understand.

AN EMPTY CLOCK
Above: One night, the Lincoln boys decided to find out how this clock worked, so they dismantled it. They were unable to put it back together.

THE CHOCOLATE LETTER
Above: In 1859, Willie Lincoln wrote this letter to his former neighbor Edward Rathbun, Jr., who stored the correspondence with some chocolates. The identity of Rathbun as the recipient was only discovered in 2011.

A Lincoln

✤ The Campaign Trail ✤

✩ ✩ ✩

Abraham Lincoln's love of politics called to him within a year after he had settled in New Salem. Though he was defeated in his first run, he went on to win four consecutive terms in the Illinois House of Representatives. He then made several attempts to secure the nomination for the United States House in the largely Democratic state, finally winning as a Whig in 1846.

In 1854, Stephen Douglas introduced a number of bills in Congress collectively known as the Kansas–Nebraska Act. Lincoln felt strongly that Douglas destroyed the Missouri Compromise of 1820 with this act, reopening the question of slavery in the territories where the Missouri Compromise had excluded it. The issue culminated in 1858, when Lincoln and Douglas discussed slavery in a series of seven debates throughout Illinois. Douglas won the United States Senate seat, but the debates made Lincoln a national figure within the new Republican Party.

In 1860, Lincoln ran for president against Douglas and two other candidates. The Southern states rejected Lincoln's anti-slavery views and his election, but the Northern states provided enough electoral votes for him to win the election. On February 11, 1861, Lincoln gave his Farewell Address to the citizens of Springfield at the Great Western Depot. Meanwhile, in Montgomery, Alabama, his old friend Alexander Stephens took the oath for the new office of Vice President of the Confederate States of America.

✤ Did You Know? ✤

Political rallies in Lincoln's day were often family events. In Monmouth, Illinois, the mother of seven-year-old Stevie Cozad made these pants so he could march in the rally with the fathers of the Fife and Drum Corps. He played his drum for Mr. Lincoln, who shook the boy's hand before starting his speech.

GRAND RALLY OF THE LINCOLN MEN OF OLD TAZEWELL!

WE HONOR THE HONEST

ABRAHAM LINCOLN.

ments of those twin cherries on a split stem, BUCHANAN and DOUGLAS of TAZEWELL and adjoining counties, are requested to assemble in **GRAND COUNCIL** at PEKIN, ON TUESDAY, OCTOBER 5TH, 1858.

ABRAHAM LINCOLN!

Will address the People at 2 o'clock, P. M. on the Political Topics of the day.

WM. KELLOGG!

HON. LYMAN TRUMBULL

President of the day, DAVID MARK, Esq.

HALF PRICE.

THE GREAT DEBATES
Above: For all the hoopla circling around the 1858 Lincoln–Douglas debates, very few mementos of that season survive. This rare broadside called out the party faithful for speeches and picnicking.

CONVENTION RIBBON
Above left: Lincoln's delegates at the 1860 Republican national convention in Chicago wore these red ribbons adorned with his photograph.

"I NOW LEAVE, NOT KNOWING WHEN, OR WHETHER EVER, I MAY RETURN, WITH A TASK BEFORE ME GREATER THAN THAT WHICH RESTED UPON WASHINGTON. WITHOUT THE ASSISTANCE OF THAT DIVINE BEING, WHO EVER ATTENDED HIM, I CANNOT SUCCEED. WITH THAT ASSISTANCE I CANNOT FAIL."

— *Abraham Lincoln, Farewell Address at the Great Western Depot in Springfield, Illinois, February 11, 1861*

A Self-Made Man

Lincoln challenged U.S. Senator Stephen A. Douglas for his seat in 1858, and nearly pulled off the upset of the decade. Lincoln's rise from flatboatman to surveyor to attorney to political figure culminated in the famous seven Lincoln-Douglas debates. The building at Knox College in Galesburg, Illinois, shown at left, is the last of the seven sites standing today. Though the campaign was grueling—Lincoln and Douglas each made at least one hundred other speeches—it launched Lincoln to national prominence.

Mrs. Lincoln's Social Circle

Mary Lincoln's transition to Washington was not easy. Most of the women in her social circle were younger, thinner, and more refined than the first lady, and they mocked her for her shortcomings. The dresses shown above are reproductions of ones worn by her rivals. Elizabeth Keckly was one of Mary Lincoln's few allies in the capital city. As Mrs. Lincoln's dressmaker and also her confidante, Keckly used her influence with the first lady to advance the cause of former slaves who resided in contraband camps around Washington, D.C. She bought her freedom—as well as her family's—by sewing dresses for Washington's elite.

❖ Life in the White House ❖

✧ ✧ ✧

Even before Abraham Lincoln took the oath of office, he faced a divided country. Despite winning a majority of the Electoral College votes, he received just 39 percent of the popular vote. (His name did not even appear on ballots cast in most Southern states.) Many Southerners, enraged by the outcome, claimed the election to be a fraud. On December 20, 1860, South Carolina seceded from the Union, declaring itself independent from the federal government. By the time Lincoln left Springfield for the White House on February 11, 1861, seven of the deep Southern states had broken from the Union to form the Confederate States of America.

Abraham Lincoln gave his first inaugural address on March 4, 1861. Although he called the secession of the Southern states "anarchy," he also used concilia-tory language. "We are not enemies, but friends," he told the gathered crowd. "We must not be enemies. Though passion may have strained, it must not break our bonds of affection." Just one month later, however, the Union would be engaged in a great Civil War.

The war was not Lincoln's only challenge. While his pioneer background and boyhood poverty distinguished him as a "man for the people" during the 1860 election, it also made him susceptible to unfair criticism during his presidency. Lincoln was widely seen as a simple-minded "railsplitter," a poor back-woodsman who was unfit for the task— far from the beloved or heroic figure that most people imagine today.

NORTH FACE OF THE EXECUTIVE MANSION
Above: Security at the White House was surprisingly lax in Lincoln's day. From the roof, Willie and Tad could see rebel flags in Virginia—and yet all the family members still spent time on the lawns.

ICONIC INKWELL
Above: Using this inkwell, Lincoln wrote his First Inaugural Address in the back room of his brother-in-law's general store in Springfield.

❖ Did You Know? ❖

The dome on the Capitol was unfinished when Lincoln gave his inaugural address. Ignoring advice to postpone further construction until after the war, Lincoln allowed the work to continue. By his second inauguration, the dome was completed along with the figure of Liberty adorning the top.

> "I HAPPEN, TEMPORARILY, TO OCCUPY THIS BIG WHITE HOUSE.
> I AM A LIVING WITNESS THAT ANY ONE OF YOUR CHILDREN MAY
> LOOK TO COME HERE AS MY FATHER'S CHILD HAS."
>
> — *Abraham Lincoln, Speech to 166th Ohio Regiment, August 22, 1864*

TAD AND ABRAHAM
Right: The youngest of the Lincoln boys, Tad was usually near his father, including on the day Alexander Gardner took this photo in 1865.

OFFICIAL AND PRIVATE CHINA
Below: Mary Lincoln chose two china patterns. For state dinners, the Lincolns used plates decorated in solferino and gold, the eagle in a roundel of clouds and sunlight; for family meals, the china had a design of buff bands within gilt spearheads and a Gothic "L," as shown on the cover of this tureen.

WILLIE'S FUNERAL SERMON
Below right: Mary Lincoln was too distraught to attend Willie's funeral, a private event in the White House. Pictured is one of three known copies of Reverend Gurley's short sermon.

FUNERAL ADDRESS

DELIVERED BY

REV. DR. GURLEY,

ON THE OCCASION OF THE

DEATH OF WILLIAM WALLACE LINCOLN.

FEBRUARY 24, 1862.

Sad and solemn is the occasion that brings us here to-day. A dark shadow of affliction has suddenly fallen upon this habitation, and upon the hearts of its inmates. The news thereof has already gone forth to the extremities of the country.

The Nation has heard it with deep and tender emotions. The eye of the Nation is moistened with tears, as it turns to-day to the Presidential Mansion; the heart of the Nation sympathizes with its Chief Magistrate, while to the unprecedented weight of civil care which presses upon him is added the burden of this great domestic sorrow; and the prayer of the Nation ascends to Heaven on his behalf, and on the behalf of his weeping family, that God's grace may be sufficient for them, and that in this hour of sore bereavement and trial, they may have the presence and succor of Him, who has said, "Come unto me all ye that labor and are heavy laden, and I will give you rest."

"SORROW COMES TO ALL . . . PERFECT RELIEF IS NOT POSSIBLE,
EXCEPT WITH TIME. YOU CAN NOT NOW REALIZE THAT YOU WILL EVER
FEEL BETTER. . . . AND YET . . . YOU ARE SURE TO BE HAPPY AGAIN."

— *Abraham Lincoln, in a condolence letter to Fanny McCullough, December 23, 1862,
on her father's death in battle, ten months after Willie Lincoln's death*

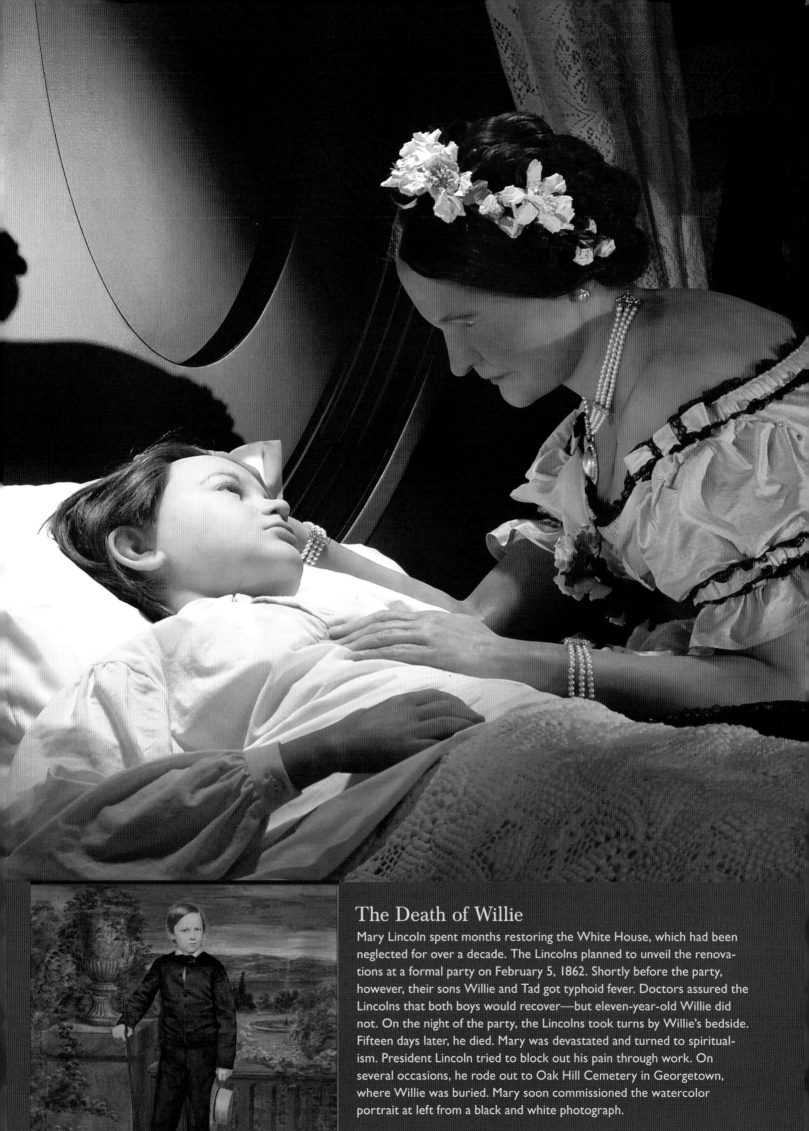

The Death of Willie

Mary Lincoln spent months restoring the White House, which had been neglected for over a decade. The Lincolns planned to unveil the renovations at a formal party on February 5, 1862. Shortly before the party, however, their sons Willie and Tad got typhoid fever. Doctors assured the Lincolns that both boys would recover—but eleven-year-old Willie did not. On the night of the party, the Lincolns took turns by Willie's bedside. Fifteen days later, he died. Mary was devastated and turned to spiritualism. President Lincoln tried to block out his pain through work. On several occasions, he rode out to Oak Hill Cemetery in Georgetown, where Willie was buried. Mary soon commissioned the watercolor portrait at left from a black and white photograph.

The Whispering Gallery

The Whispering Gallery highlights the pressures that the Lincolns faced, using a mix of audio tracks of unfavorable comments about the president and first lady that were taken from contemporary diaries, newspapers, and letters. All presidents face the harpoons of cartoonists, but Lincoln was especially hated for being an uneducated Westerner, supposedly a warmonger—and even for getting re-elected.

COLUMBIA'S NIGHTMARE.

Run Abe for your life— the Blood tubs are after yer !!!

(1.) THE ALARM.

"MY MARYLAND!!!"

THE OVERDUE BILL.

OLD ABE—"Oh, it's all well enough to say, that I must support the dignity of my high office by Force—but it's darned uncomfortable sitting—I can tell yer."

ONE KIND OF PATRIOTISM.

America's Bloodiest War

This 2005 mural by Danilo Montejo, above, depicts the battle at Fort Sumter. Although there were no casualties at Fort Sumter, the skirmish ignited furor on both sides, releasing decades of anger over the issue of slavery. The Northern states rallied behind President Lincoln, while Virginia, Arkansas, North Carolina, and Tennessee joined the Confederate states. In the early months of the war, most people believed there would be little bloodshed. However, the first battle of Bull Run (Manassas), on July 21, 1861, dispelled that notion. There, a total of nearly 900 men were killed and 2,600 were wounded—setting the stage for what would become the nation's bloodiest war.

⚜ Early Civil War ⚜

⚜ ⚜ ⚜

By early 1861, Fort Sumter, in the harbor of Charleston, South Carolina, was one of the few federal garrisons in the South not yet seized by rebels. About eighty-five federal troops occupied the fort. The Confederate army called for the Union to surrender the fort, but the Union commander of the garrison refused—so on April 12, 1861, Confederate troops began to fire on Fort Sumter. President Lincoln acted decisively. He called up seventy-five thousand state militia troops, purchased supplies, and declared a blockade against Southern ports even though he lacked a navy large enough to make it effective. Suddenly, the civil war that most people hoped would never occur gripped the country.

Southerners believed they were leading another revolution. Northerners, however, saw the war as a struggle for two different causes: a military war to preserve the Union, and a war for emancipation and freedom for slaves. Lincoln turned to key people for help on both fronts. His initial trust in General George McClellan turned to frustration when McClellan repeatedly failed to destroy the rebel army. After mid-1863, it was General Ulysses S. Grant who provided Lincoln with the military victories that eventually won the war. Several black Americans also assisted in the cause: Frederick Douglass, undoubtedly the most influential black abolitionist editor, had meetings with Lincoln that were later detailed in his autobiography; and abolitionist Sojourner Truth worked tirelessly to enlist black troops.

BATTLE OF BULL RUN
Left: This section of a 12 x 5 ½ foot painting by James Paul Servar, painted in 1919 when he was seventy-nine, depicts the first face-to-face battle of the war.

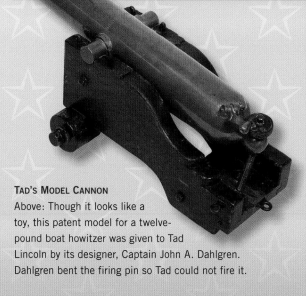

TAD'S MODEL CANNON
Above: Though it looks like a toy, this patent model for a twelve-pound boat howitzer was given to Tad Lincoln by its designer, Captain John A. Dahlgren. Dahlgren bent the firing pin so Tad could not fire it.

⚜ Did You Know? ⚜

The younger Lincoln boys, Willie and Tad, found the war news exciting and talked every day with the soldiers who guarded the White House. The War Department made Tad an honorary lieutenant, as seen at right. Robert Lincoln, Abraham and Mary's eldest, was officially a captain on the staff of General Ulysses Grant in the last months of the war.

"THOSE WHO DENY FREEDOM TO OTHERS DESERVE IT NOT FOR THEMSELVES, AND, UNDER A JUST GOD, CANNOT LONG RETAIN IT."

— *Abraham Lincoln, in a letter to H. L. Pierce, April 6, 1859*

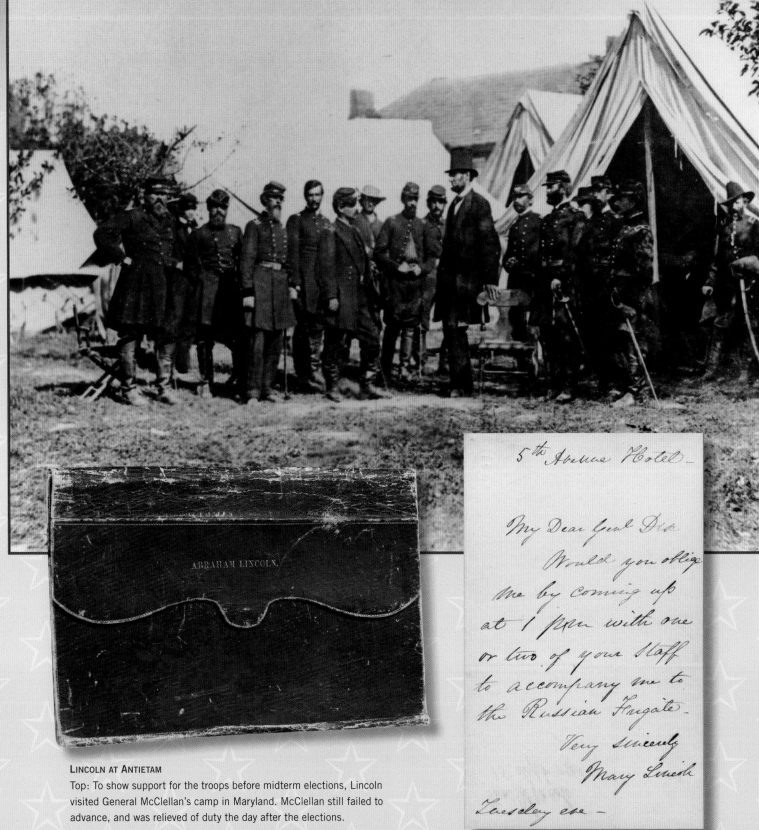

LINCOLN AT ANTIETAM
Top: To show support for the troops before midterm elections, Lincoln visited General McClellan's camp in Maryland. McClellan still failed to advance, and was relieved of duty the day after the elections.

LINCOLN'S BRIEFCASE
Above: In this leather portfolio Lincoln carried papers to and from his cottage at the Soldiers' Home (in the north part of Washington) each night during the summers. Red wax still smears the inside of the flap.

MARY LINCOLN AND THE WAR
Above: In 1863, Russian naval ships arrived unannounced in New York Harbor to show support for Union troops. In this letter, Mary Lincoln asked General John A. Dix to accompany her on a formal visit to the officers.

"THE OCCASION IS PILED HIGH WITH DIFFICULTY, AND WE MUST RISE WITH THE OCCASION. AS OUR CASE IS NEW, SO WE MUST THINK ANEW, AND ACT ANEW. WE MUST DISENTHRALL OURSELVES, AND THEN WE SHALL SAVE OUR COUNTRY."

— *Abraham Lincoln, December 1, 1862, Message to Congress*

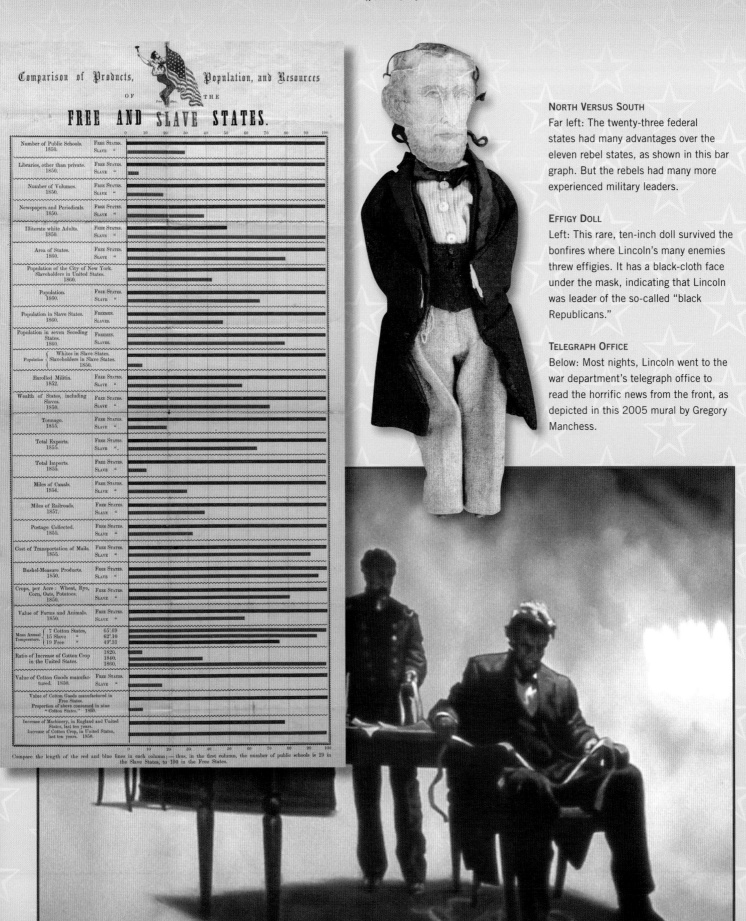

Comparison of Products, Population, and Resources OF THE

FREE AND SLAVE STATES.

Compare the length of the red and blue lines in each column:—thus, in the first column, the number of public schools is 29 in the Slave States, to 100 in the Free States.

NORTH VERSUS SOUTH

Far left: The twenty-three federal states had many advantages over the eleven rebel states, as shown in this bar graph. But the rebels had many more experienced military leaders.

EFFIGY DOLL

Left: This rare, ten-inch doll survived the bonfires where Lincoln's many enemies threw effigies. It has a black-cloth face under the mask, indicating that Lincoln was leader of the so-called "black Republicans."

TELEGRAPH OFFICE

Below: Most nights, Lincoln went to the war department's telegraph office to read the horrific news from the front, as depicted in this 2005 mural by Gregory Manchess.

A Lincoln

❖ The War Gallery ❖

The War Gallery presents scores of images of the Civil War, along with displays and interactive exhibits that illustrate the human tragedy and sacrifice that occurred. It also follows the stories of four ordinary Union and four Confederate soldiers, and includes uniform reproductions, letters, and pictures.

7th Illinois Infantry Color Bearers

A Political Freedom Fighter

Once issued, the Emancipation Proclamation sent shockwaves through the nation. On numerous occasions, Lincoln—shown above reading the proclamation to his cabinet—was urged to revoke it. He often replied by stating, "Broken eggs cannot be mended," meaning that action taken could not be undone. Lincoln wrote in one letter to a Union general: "I think I shall not retract or repudiate it. Those who shall have tasted actual freedom I believe can never be slaves or quasi slaves again." The A. H. Ritchie engraving at right, based on the 1864 painting by Francis Carpenter, shows Lincoln's cabinet discussing the proclamation. Carpenter lived in the White House for six months to accurately render the scene.

A. Lincoln

Emancipation Proclamation

On July 22, 1862, President Lincoln called a cabinet meeting in his office to read a preliminary draft of his Emancipation Proclamation. The proclamation stated that the slaves in all rebel-held territory would be declared free as of January 1, 1863. Some cabinet members favored it; others thought it would undermine Republican candidates in the midterm elections. Secretary of State William Henry Seward advised the president not to issue the proclamation until after a Union military victory. Otherwise, European nations might view the new policy as a desperate act stemming from weakness rather than from a position of moral and military strength. Lincoln agreed, and found his moment after General McClellan halted Robert E. Lee's invasion of Maryland at Antietam on September 17, 1862.

Lincoln believed that the Emancipation Proclamation was his most important state paper. Using his war powers as commander-in-chief, he issued it as an executive order. As long as the war raged, the executive order remained in effect. His decision indicated that the war for union was now also a war for emancipation and freedom. It encouraged blacks in the North to enlist in the Union army or navy, and ordered the officers to accept those volunteers. Lincoln then set to work on making the order permanent through an amendment to the Constitution.

SPECTACLES
Below: Sometimes Lincoln wore modern spectacles for what he called his "old eyes"; other times, he used these *pince-nez* eyeglasses (French for "pinch-nose").

SIGNED "EMANCIPATION"
Above: Lincoln's original manuscript of the Emancipation Proclamation was burned in the Chicago Fire of 1871. This rare signed copy of the printed text is on display at the Museum on special occasions.

CHOPPING DOWN SLAVERY
Above: One cartoonist melded Lincoln's legendary power with an ax with his hatred of slavery.

"IN GIVING FREEDOM TO THE SLAVE,
WE ASSURE FREEDOM TO THE FREE—HONORABLE ALIKE
IN WHAT WE GIVE AND WHAT WE PRESERVE."

— *Abraham Lincoln, Annual Message to Congress, December 1, 1862*

A. Lincoln

⊰ The Civil War in Four Minutes ⊱

The War Gallery features a film called *The Civil War in Four Minutes*, in which each week of the war is condensed to one second. An electronic map rolls nonstop, moving battle lines to depict the war's changing progress, while a casualty counter tracks the mounting numbers of the wounded or dead.

A. Lincoln

CASUALTIES
NORTH 27
SOUTH 20

June 9, 1861

CASUALTIES
NORTH 370,533
SOUTH 331,389

July 9, 1863

CASUALTIES
NORTH 702,000
SOUTH 621,000

May 30, 1865

CASUALTIES
NORTH 639,333
SOUTH 529,323

October 19, 1864

A SOLDIER'S STORY

A. Lincoln

❧ The Battle of Gettysburg ❧

✧ ✧ ✧

In the summer of 1863, Robert E. Lee marched his army into Pennsylvania, attempting to create fear and uncertainty in an already war-weary population. His efforts were repulsed in heavy fighting at the town of Gettysburg. The three-day Battle of Gettysburg represented a turning point in the Civil War: After winning several successive battles, the Confederacy was finally put on the defensive, and the Union began to gain momentum. Gettysburg also claimed fifty-one thousand casualties—representing those who died, were injured, or were captured. It was the largest battle ever fought on American soil.

The huge number of dead threatened an outbreak of disease, requiring the federal government to establish a national military cemetery at the site. Edward Everett, a former secretary of state and a president of Harvard College, was the featured speaker. As a capstone, President Lincoln was asked to make a few appropriate remarks. In his Gettysburg oration, Lincoln described the blood sacrifice of soldiers who died and how their lives could be honored by bringing a new birth of freedom to the United States. The Gettysburg Address, which lasted about two minutes, was ignored or mocked by much of the media. Today, it is one of the best-known speeches in American history.

LINCOLN AT GETTYSBURG
Above right: Lincoln's face was barely captured in this photograph from the Gettysburg cemetery dedication ceremonies. He can be seen just left of the tall man standing at center.

WALKING STICK
Right: Senator John Conness of California presented this cane to Lincoln in late 1863, shortly before the speech at Gettysburg, as a tribute to his work toward emancipation. It is made of California oak and Gold Rush gold, and is elegantly inscribed.

❧ Did You Know? ❧

Lincoln's personal attendant and friend William Johnson (who was "colored," as it says on this note) rode with the family from Springfield to Washington. He also traveled with Lincoln to Gettysburg, and was standing by while Lincoln finished writing his great address. Johnson died of smallpox six weeks later, and Lincoln paid for his burial and marker at Arlington National Cemetery. His marker there still stands. No photo of Johnson exists—only some notes and checks written to him from Lincoln.

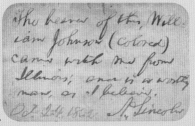

"WE HERE HIGHLY RESOLVE THAT THESE DEAD SHALL NOT HAVE DIED IN VAIN—THAT THIS NATION, UNDER GOD, SHALL HAVE A NEW BIRTH OF FREEDOM—AND THAT GOVERNMENT OF THE PEOPLE, BY THE PEOPLE, FOR THE PEOPLE, SHALL NOT PERISH FROM THE EARTH."

— *Abraham Lincoln, Gettysburg Address, November 19, 1863*

Presidential Pressures

This 2005 mural by Keith Rocco, above, shows President Lincoln giving the Gettysburg Address. While Lincoln is now remembered as a great orator and leader, as president he received numerous death threats. He also struggled to lead a country that was becoming more fractured each day. As the number of casualties continued to grow, so did the public's frustration at the toll the war was taking on the country. Lincoln often expressed his concerns to friends and colleagues. In November 1863, he wrote to Republican Senator Zachariah Chandler: "I hope to 'stand firm' enough not to go backward, and yet not go forward fast enough to wreck the country's cause." One year later, he told a veteran abolitionist, "This war is eating my life out. I have a strong impression that I shall not live to see the end."

A. Lincoln

❧ The Gettysburg Address ❧

✦ ✦ ✦

Lincoln was justly proud of his most famous speech. Five written versions of it survive today: Two incomplete drafts are in the Library of Congress; one version that was rejected by a book publisher is at Cornell University (the publisher had asked for the speech to be written on three pages rather than two); and one with a title, date, and signature now hangs in the Lincoln bedroom of the White House. The Presidential Museum has the address pictured here, which Lincoln wrote out for Edward Everett. It was to be sold for charity along with Everett's souvenir notebook of the day, and is the first place where "under God" appears in the phrase "that this nation, under God."

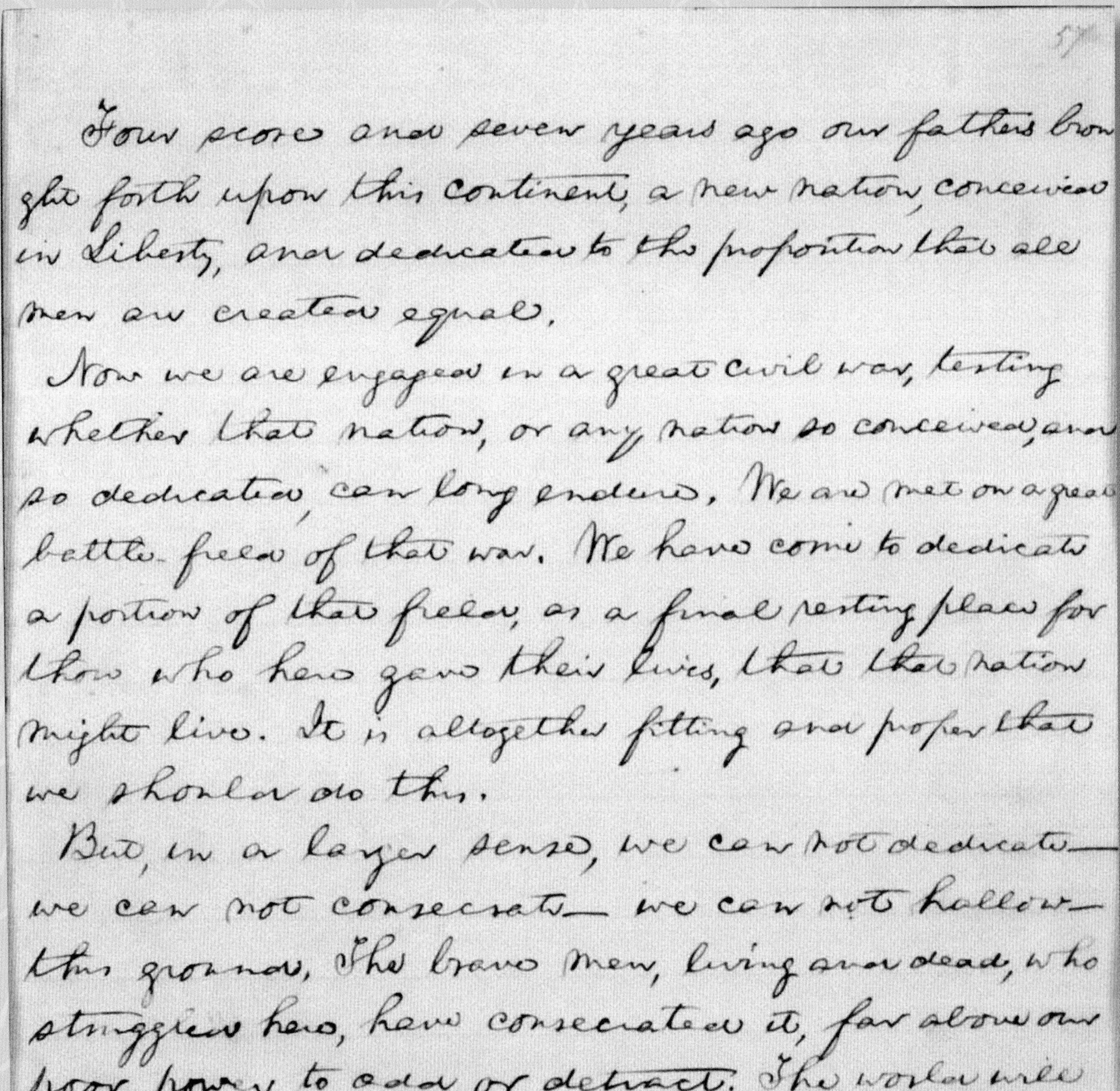

> Four score and seven years ago our fathers brought forth upon this continent, a new nation, conceived in Liberty, and dedicated to the proposition that all men are created equal.
>
> Now we are engaged in a great civil war, testing whether that nation, or any nation so conceived, and so dedicated, can long endure. We are met on a great battle-field of that war. We have come to dedicate a portion of that field, as a final resting place for those who here gave their lives, that that nation might live. It is altogether fitting and proper that we should do this.
>
> But, in a larger sense, we can not dedicate— we can not consecrate— we can not hallow— this ground. The brave men, living and dead, who struggled here, have consecrated it, far above our poor power to add or detract. The world will little note, nor long remember, what we say here, but it can never forget what they did here. It is for us, the living, rather, to be dedicated here to the unfinished work which they who fought here, have, thus far, so nobly advanced. It is rather for us to be here dedicated to the great task remaining before

A. Lincoln

58

us— that from these honored dead we take increas= er devotion to that cause for which they here gave the last full measure of devotion— that we here highly resolve that these dead shall not have died in vain— that this nation, under God, shall have a new birth of freedom— and that, government of the people, by the people, for the people, shall not perish from the earth.

THE "GETTYSBURG PHOTOGRAPH"
Below: This unique picture of Lincoln looking straight at the camera was taken by Alexander Gardner just eleven days before the great speech, and so is identified with that event.

EVERETT'S NOTEBOOK
Below left and below: Everett sent Lincoln two leaves of blue-lined paper on which to write his address. Everett numbered them "57" and "58" (in the upper-right corners) for inclusion in his notebook. Everett's notebook—which was sold for charity—included some of his manuscript notes, battle maps, and pictures of generals, and ended with Lincoln's manuscript.

ADDRESS AT GETTYSBURG BY EDWARD EVERETT, MS.

Major General Meade.

Manuscript of the Address Delivered at the Consecration of the National Cemetery at Gettysburg on the 19th of November 1863 together with the Manuscript of President Lincoln's dedicatory Speech on the same occasion.

THE 13TH AMENDMENT   THE 2ND INAUGURAL   THE FALL OF RICHMOND   PLAY PEN   LAST SPEECH

The Thirteenth Amendment

Once Lincoln as Commander had emancipated the slaves in rebel territory, he began to work on the constitutional, permanent version of that policy. The Thirteenth Amendment to the U.S. Constitution, which banned slavery forever, passed the U.S. Senate in April 1864. After enormous politicking and lobbying, the House passed it in January 1865. (The original document with his signature is seen here.) Then the amendment went to the states for ratification, becoming law in December 1865. In death, Lincoln's wish was finally complete.

A. Lincoln

❧ The Tide Turns ❧

After weeks of siege warfare, on September 2, 1864, Major General William Tecumseh Sherman captured Atlanta, Georgia, providing a major Union victory for the war-weary North. Drawing upon that victory, Lincoln won the vote in the November presidential election. His re-election meant there would be no compromise with the Confederate government on abolishing slavery. Yet Lincoln knew that only a constitutional amendment could guarantee that blacks would keep the freedom obtained by the war. Shortly after his re-election, he secured enough votes to pass the Thirteenth Amendment through Congress, on January 31, 1865.

On the wet and windy morning of March 4, 1865, President Lincoln took his second oath of office. He encouraged the nation, stating, "Fondly do we hope—fervently do we pray—that this mighty scourge of war may speedily pass away."

The war finally ended on April 9, 1865, when General Lee surrendered to General Grant in the rural town of Appomattox Court House, Virginia. An estimated 620,000 lives were lost on both sides over the course of four years, and more than one-quarter of all Southern white men were dead. The war was the bloodiest in the nation's history, but it ended the torment of slavery once and for all.

CAMPAIGN LANTERN
Left: Rusty and fragile, this 1864 glass campaign lantern—used for nighttime rallies—has somehow survived the years.

LINCOLN AND JOHNSON CAMPAIGN FLAG
Above left: Andrew Johnson was the only Southern senator to remain loyal to the Union, and Lincoln felt that this bravery deserved a spot on the 1864 Union ticket.

MYRIOPTICON
Left: This 1864 tabletop game depicts a dozen scenes from the war along a turning scroll.

"WITH MALICE TOWARD NONE; WITH CHARITY FOR ALL; WITH FIRMNESS IN THE RIGHT, AS GOD GIVES US TO SEE THE RIGHT, LET US STRIVE ON TO FINISH THE WORK WE ARE IN; TO BIND UP THE NATION'S WOUNDS."

— Abraham Lincoln, Second Inaugural Address, March 4, 1865

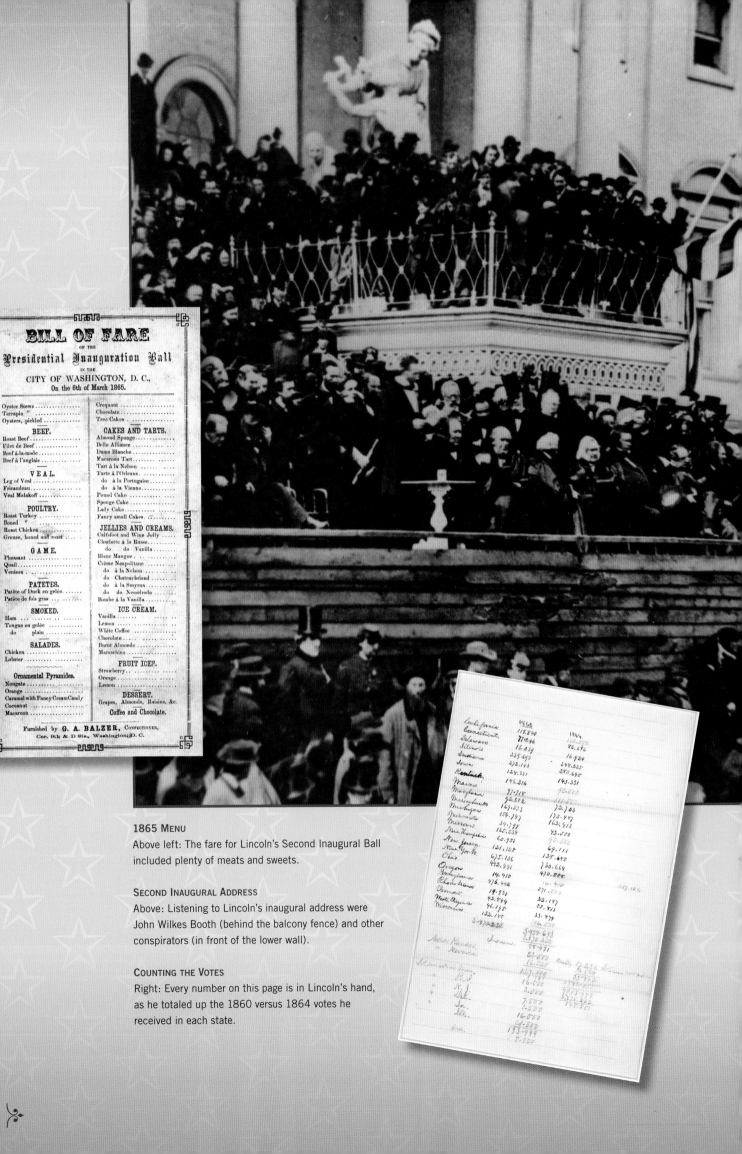

1865 MENU
Above left: The fare for Lincoln's Second Inaugural Ball included plenty of meats and sweets.

SECOND INAUGURAL ADDRESS
Above: Listening to Lincoln's inaugural address were John Wilkes Booth (behind the balcony fence) and other conspirators (in front of the lower wall).

COUNTING THE VOTES
Right: Every number on this page is in Lincoln's hand, as he totaled up the 1860 versus 1864 votes he received in each state.

❊ Did You Know? ❊

A symbol of Lincoln's rail-splitting youth and a campaign image for his 1860 presidential bid, the ax remains associated with Abraham Lincoln almost as much as his stovepipe hat. This ax stood by a woodpile at General Grant's camp in Virginia during Lincoln's visit in April 1865. Wounded soldiers asked him to demonstrate his Illinois experience with it. Lincoln picked it up and chopped the wood for their fires that night; then he held it perpendicular to his body in a muscle-man show of strength. One week later, he was killed.

LINCOLN AND GRANT
Above: Lincoln sent Ulysses S. Grant—pictured at top—"the nation's grateful thanks" for his victories in Virginia. Grant deserves much credit for Lincoln's fame today.

ROBERT E. LEE
Left: Though Confederate commander Robert E. Lee was the stronger student at West Point, he was beaten by fellow West Point graduate Ulysses S. Grant in the end.

"WE MEET THIS EVENING, NOT IN SORROW, BUT IN GLADNESS OF HEART. THE EVACUATION OF PETERSBURG AND RICHMOND, AND THE SURRENDER OF THE PRINCIPAL INSURGENT ARMY, GIVE HOPE OF A RIGHTEOUS AND SPEEDY PEACE WHOSE JOYOUS EXPRESSION CAN NOT BE RESTRAINED."

— *Abraham Lincoln, Last Public Address, April 11, 1865*

The Plot to Kill Lincoln

John Wilkes Booth and several other conspirators had planned to kill Ulysses S. Grant as well as President Lincoln, but Grant was not at the theater that night. (Plans to kill two other key politicians also failed.) Booth had performed several times at Ford's Theatre and knew the layout of the building well. About an hour after Lincoln's bodyguard had left his post to have a drink at a nearby tavern, Booth entered Lincoln's box and shot the president. Booth did not get far after leaving the theater: Many theatergoers recognized him, and a massive manhunt took place. Soldiers found Booth and another conspirator at a tobacco farm in Virginia twelve days later, and one of them mortally shot Booth in the neck.

The Passing of a President

Lincoln was not able to enjoy the Union's victory for long. On April 11, 1865, he gave a speech from an upper window of the White House, while white supremacist and actor John Wilkes Booth stood below. Booth turned to a companion and vowed, "That will be the last speech he will ever make."

Just three days later, the Lincolns—who were frequent theatergoers—attended the British comedy *Our American Cousin.* Some newspapers announced that the president and the first lady would be in attendance. Major Henry Rathbone and his fiancée Clara Harris, daughter of New York Senator Ira Harris, were the Lincolns' guests. During the third act, Booth entered the Lincolns' box and waited for the loudest laugh line in the play. Then he shot the president point-blank in the back of the skull. Lincoln slumped forward while Major Rathbone struggled to detain the assassin. Booth cut Rathbone's arm with a huge knife and then jumped from the box approximately ten feet to the stage, breaking his ankle. Straightening himself, he yelled the state motto of Virginia, "*Sic semper tyrannus!*" a Latin phrase that means "Thus always to tyrants." Lincoln's limp body was carried across the street to a boardinghouse. There he died at 7:22 a.m. on April 15, 1865.

FORD'S THEATRE
Left: The Lincolns attended Ford's Theatre on many occasions. Some of their happiest times were watching a show together.

Did You Know?

The structure of Ford's Theatre was built as a church. In the fall of 1861, John T. Ford converted it to a theater. Aside from enduring a fire the next year, the theater was very successful. It became a popular destination for the Washington crowd of soldiers, government workers, and visitors— until Lincoln's assassination in April 1865. Ford tried to reopen the theater but was prevented by public outrage. The War Department purchased it from him in 1866.

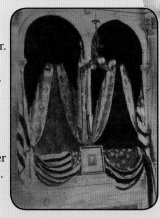

BLOOD-STAINED GLOVES
Above: Lincoln's kid-leather gloves became stained with his blood after he was shot.

"I WOULD RATHER BE ASSASSINATED ON THIS SPOT THAN TO SURRENDER [THE PRINCIPLES OF THE DECLARATION OF INDEPENDENCE]."

— *Abraham Lincoln, speaking in Independence Hall, February 22, 1861*

BOOTH AT THE DOOR
Left: Booth had drilled a tiny eyehole that allowed him to see his target before entering the box.

THE LEAPING ESCAPE
Below: This rare, hand-colored, and highly inaccurate illustration of the deed depicts Lincoln standing up.

SOUVENIR CARD
Below left: Myriad cards and photos were sold after Lincoln's assassination. This one depicts the devil whispering to Booth as he ponders his plot to kill the president.

THE ASSASSINATION OF PRESIDENT LINCOLN

MARY'S BLOOD-STAINED FAN
Left: Made of ivory sticks, silk blades, and ostrich-feather tips, Mary Lincoln's fan was closed at the time of the assassination. Only its far right blade was stained, probably with Major Rathbone's blood.

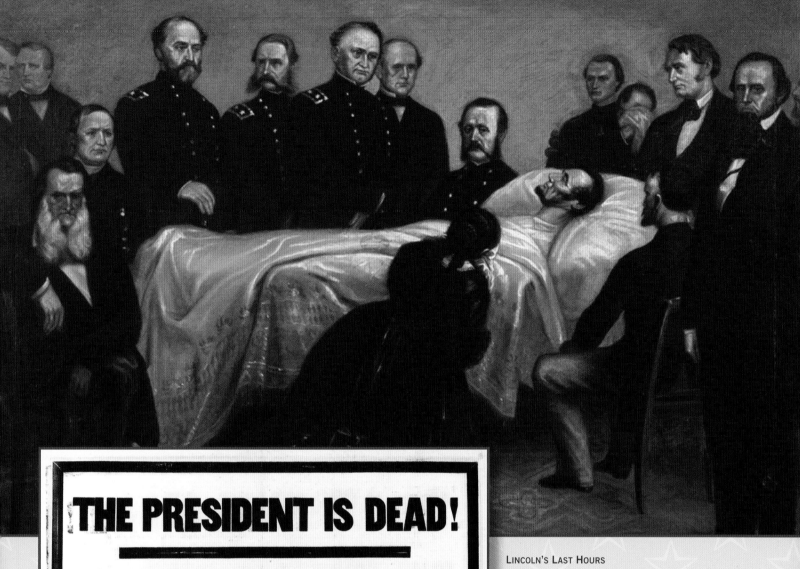

THE PRESIDENT IS DEAD!

WAR DEPARTMENT,
Washington, April 15, 1865.

To MAJ. GEN. DIX,
Abraham Lincoln died this morning at 22 minutes af
Seven o'clock.
E. M. STANTON, Sec. of Wa

LINCOLN'S LAST HOURS
Above: In 1867, with lustrous oils and moving emotion, German-born artist Peter Kramer painted over his lithograph of the deathbed scene. In reality, only about six or seven visitors at a time could fit into the little room in the Petersen house.

OFFICIAL DEATH NOTICE
Above: Edwin M. Stanton said at Lincoln's bedside, "Now he belongs to the ages," then sent telegrams to all military districts.

LAURA KEENE'S DRESS
Right: Laura Keene, the play's starring actress, rushed from the stage up to Lincoln's box and cradled his head while a doctor probed his wound. She presented this bloody piece of her dress to the builders of Lincoln's tomb the next year.

A Nation in Mourning

Abraham Lincoln's death had a profound effect on the nation. Many Northerners believed the assassination to be part of a wider Confederate plot, and dozens of Southern sympathizers were beaten, tarred, and in some cases killed. Across the country, flags flew at half-mast, and the doors of houses were draped in black crepe. During Easter services that Sunday, many Northern churches compared the shooting (which had occurred on Good Friday) to the crucifixion of Christ—inspiring a widespread reverence for the president that had barely begun during his lifetime. Edwin Stanton confiscated this unique photo of Lincoln in his casket, right, in New York's City Hall. It was rediscovered in 1952.

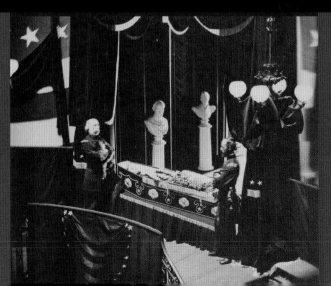

A. Lincoln

☆ Holding on to Lincoln ☆

☆ ☆ ☆

Abraham Lincoln's death, which marked the first assassination of a U.S. president, stunned the already war-weary nation. A Treasury deputy hastily planned memorial services in Washington, D.C., while Secretary of War Edwin Stanton arranged an elaborate funeral train that retraced the route Lincoln had taken to his first inauguration. The 1,662-mile procession, which traveled from April 21 to May 3, wound through eleven major cities as it transported the president's remains back to Springfield, Illinois. At each major city, Lincoln's casket was removed from the train, and the public paid its respects. In Springfield, a city of perhaps fifteen thousand residents, more than seventy-five thousand people passed by Lincoln's open casket in a twenty-four-hour period.

As people walked by Lincoln's remains, they often took small mementos from the floral displays or mourning decorations. Some of these objects were passed down through generations and are on display at the Museum today. Among them are the silver spoon Elizabeth Keckly saved from Lincoln's last meal, train schedules from Lincoln's funeral procession, and tassels from the fringe of the casket.

NEW YORK FUNERAL
Far left: New York's City Hall is one of the only funeral sites still standing today.

TIMETABLE FOR OHIO
Left: Detailed schedules were distributed across the country so that families could stand by the tracks as the train stopped or passed by.

FUNERAL CARRIAGE
Above: Horses pulled the carriage and caskets carrying Lincoln and Willie to Oak Ridge Cemetery in Springfield. The carriage was trailed by a two-mile procession of mourners.

☆ Did You Know? ☆

Abraham Lincoln's funeral train, which consisted of nine cars, also carried the remains of his son Willie. Mrs. Lincoln was too distraught to join the funeral procession and could not even bring herself to leave the White House for five weeks.

"EVERY MAN IS SAID TO HAVE HIS PECULIAR AMBITION. WHETHER IT BE TRUE OR NOT, I CAN SAY FOR ONE THAT I HAVE NO OTHER SO GREAT AS THAT OF BEING TRULY ESTEEMED OF MY FELLOW MEN, BY RENDERING MYSELF WORTHY OF THEIR ESTEEM."

— *Abraham Lincoln, Handbill for the People of Sangamo County, March 9, 1832*

❊ The Gateway ❊

There are many sites throughout the country that celebrate Lincoln's legacy. The Museum's entry and exit point, the Gateway, highlights other Lincoln attractions, including his birthplace cabin in Kentucky, boyhood home in Indiana, and law office in Springfield, as well as the Gettysburg National Cemetery in Pennsylvania and sites in Washington, D.C. Any Lincoln, Illinois history, or genealogical topic can be researched for free at the Presidential Library across the street.

To encourage visitors to explore historic sites in Illinois and other places, the Museum displays "Looking for Lincoln" wall plaques, which feature directions to these locations. Approximately two dozen communities in Illinois developed the "Looking for Lincoln" program. These communities—all with special connections to the former president—have events throughout the year that celebrate Abraham Lincoln. They also feature a number of historic markers that provide detailed information about Lincoln's friends, his political and legal activities, and his other connections to the community.

Many of these activities are designed for children. For example, Springfield offers a walking tour in its historic district, where families can follow "Looking for Lincoln" plaques. Kids can bring paper and crayons, and make rubbings from the unique medallions on each sign. They can also go to www.lookingforlincoln.org and download plans for Lincoln-era buildings that can be printed out on heavy paper and folded to create their own village.

OLD STATE CAPITOL
Above: Here Lincoln gave his "House Divided" speech in June 1858, and here he lay in state in May 1865.

THE BERRY–LINCOLN STORE
Above: This site in New Salem is one of two dozen re-created cabins from the 1830s. Located about twenty miles from Springfield, New Salem gives visitors the best sense of Lincoln's humble beginnings and big dreams.

❊ Did You Know? ❊

The only home the Lincolns ever owned was located on the corner of 8th and Jackson in Springfield. When Lincoln purchased the home in 1844 for $1,500, the house was a small one-and-a-half story cottage. Over the years, the Lincolns made many improvements. Today, the home is a popular National Historic Site.

"MY FRIENDS, NO ONE, NOT IN MY SITUATION, CAN APPRECIATE MY FEELING OF SADNESS AT THIS PARTING. TO THIS PLACE, AND THE KINDNESS OF THESE PEOPLE, I OWE EVERYTHING."

— *Abraham Lincoln, Farewell Address at the Great Western Depot in Springfield, Illinois, February 11, 1861*

Looking for Lincoln

In 2008, Congress enacted legislation to designate forty-two counties in central Illinois as the Abraham Lincoln National Heritage Area—the nation's only Heritage Area named for an American president. The area is managed by the Looking for Lincoln Heritage Coalition, a nonprofit corporation that informs and educates visitors on the life of America's sixteenth president. The fifty-two communities that make up this area highlight the three decades in which Lincoln lived in central Illinois. Each has at least one Story Trail, a wayside exhibit with more information about Lincoln's life. There are more than two hundred wayside exhibits in all.

IN THIS TEMPLE
AS IN THE HEARTS OF THE PEOPLE
FOR WHOM HE SAVED THE UNION
THE MEMORY OF ABRAHAM LINCOLN
IS ENSHRINED FOREVER

Carved in Stone

Abraham Lincoln's statue in the Lincoln Memorial—which weighs
175 tons—took four years to carve. The likeness was originally slated
to be ten feet tall, but was built to be much taller (nineteen feet high)
in order to avoid being dwarfed by the chamber in which it sits. Carved
inscriptions from Lincoln's most famous speeches, the Gettysburg
Address and his Second Inaugural Address, can be seen along the south
and north chambers of the memorial. This postcard of the then-new
Memorial, right, was mailed to a friend in Illinois in 1923.

A. Lincoln

⊰ The Lincoln Memorial ⊱

"In this temple, as in the hearts of the people for whom he saved the Union, the memory of Abraham Lincoln is enshrined forever." These words are written above a marble likeness of the sixteenth President of the United States, which stands at the west end of the National Mall in Washington, D.C.

The sculpture of Lincoln was created by Daniel Chester French, and the architect Henry Bacon designed the Memorial. Construction began on the Lincoln Memorial in 1914, and it was dedicated in 1922—a joyous celebration of the country's reunification after the Civil War. Robert Lincoln, the Lincolns' only surviving son, attended the dedication. He received a standing ovation when he reached his seat. Over time, the memorial became the site of many civil rights demonstrations. African American opera singer Marian Anderson performed for seventy-five thousand people at the memorial on Easter Sunday in 1939. And Martin Luther King, Jr., gave his famous "I Have a Dream" speech in front of two hundred thousand people in 1963. In 2003, the National Park Service inscribed the words "I have a dream" on the steps where King stood at the Lincoln Memorial. In 2009, the government held a rededication retrospective on the bicentennial of Abraham Lincoln's birth. Today, the memorial is one of the most popular landmarks in the nation's capital, an inspiring symbol of freedom to the millions of people who tour it each year.

A RARE APPEARANCE
Left: Robert Lincoln politely turned down hundreds of requests to speak or appear, but he and his wife, Mary, attended the 1922 dedication of the Memorial.

IN OUR POCKETS
Left and far left: Lincoln's legacy is so vast that we sometimes forget that nearly every American carries his image every day—since 1909 on the penny, since 1914 on the $5 bill, or on one of four stamps from 2009.

"FOUR SCORE AND SEVEN YEARS AGO OUR FATHERS BROUGHT FORTH UPON THIS CONTINENT, A NEW NATION, CONCEIVED IN LIBERTY, AND DEDICATED TO THE PROPOSITION THAT ALL MEN ARE CREATED EQUAL."
— *Abraham Lincoln, Gettysburg Address, November 19, 1863*

ABRAHAM LINCOLN
PRESIDENTIAL LIBRARY & MUSEUM

America's most-visited Presidential Library and Museum opened in 2005 and has welcomed more than 4.1 million visitors since. The Lincoln Collection—begun in the predecessor Illinois State Historical Library—numbers fifty-two thousand items, while the entire collection on Illinois and national history counts more than twelve million items. The non-profit Presidential Library Foundation, formed to support educational and cultural programming, seeks "to foster Lincoln scholarship through the acquisition and publication of documentary materials relating to Lincoln and his era; and to promote a greater appreciation of history through exhibits, conferences, publications, online services, and other activities designed to promote historical literacy."

Text by Thomas F. Schwartz, with assistance from James M. Cornelius. Special thanks to Jennifer Ericson and Dave Blanchette for work on the images.

Abraham Lincoln Presidential Library and Museum
212 North Sixth Street
Springfield, IL 62701
www.alplm.org
(800) 610-2094
(217) 782-5764

BECKON BOOKS

Abraham Lincoln Presidential Library and Museum: Official Commemorative Guide was developed by Beckon Books in cooperation with the Abraham Lincoln Presidential Library and Museum and Event Network. Beckon develops and publishes custom books for leading cultural attractions, corporations, and non-profit organizations. Beckon Books is an imprint of Southwestern Publishing Group, Inc., 2451 Atrium Way, Nashville, TN 37214. Southwestern Publishing Group, Inc., is a wholly owned subsidiary of Southwestern, Inc., Nashville, Tennessee.

Christopher G. Capen, *President, Beckon Books*
Monika Stout, *Design/Production*
Betsy Holt, *Editor*
www.beckonbooks.com
877-311-0155

Event Network is the retail partner of the Abraham Lincoln Presidential Library and Museum, and is proud to benefit and support the Museum's mission to educate visitors on the life and times of Abraham Lincoln. www.eventnetwork.com

ISBN: 978-1-935442-13-4
Printed in China
10 9 8 7 6 5 4 3

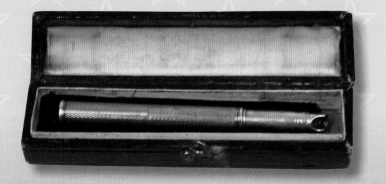

From His Desk: Lincoln's rise as a self-made man is captured by two items found on his desk the day he died: the simple goose-quill pen of his youth, and this 14-karat-gold reversible pen/pencil that was given to the Library and Museum in 2011.